To my mom: thanks for making me eat my vegetables

ABOUT THIS BOOK

The illustrations for this book were done in watercolor, ink, and colored pencil on 140lb cold-press paper. This book was edited by Nikki Garcia and designed by Véronique Lefèvre Sweet. The production was supervised by Patricia Alvarado, and the production editor was Marisa Finkelstein. The text was set in Triplex, and the display type is Fontesque Bold and and Sharee Miller's hand-lettered font.

Little, Brown and Company
Hachette Book Group
1290 Avenue of the Americas, New York, NY 10104
Visit us at LBYR.com

First Edition: March 2021

Little, Brown and Company is a division of Hachette Book Group, Inc.
The Little, Brown name and logo are trademarks of Hachette Book Group, Inc.

The publisher is not responsible for websites (or their content) that are not owned by the publisher.

Photograph of Michelle Obama and children © U.S. Department of Agriculture/Flickr

Library of Congress Cataloging-in-Publication Data
Names: Miller, Sharee (Illustrator), author.
Title: Michelle's garden: how the first lady planted seeds of change / Sharee Miller.
Description: First edition. | New York, NY: Little, Brown and Company, 2020. | Audience: Ages 4–8 |
Summary: "The story of Michelle Obama and her time in the White House, where she led in the growth of a kitchen garden" —Provided by publisher.
Identifiers: LCCN 2020005058 | ISBN 9780316458573 (hardcover)
Subjects: LCSH: Obama, Michelle, 1964——Juvenile literature. | Kitchen gardens—Juvenile literature. | Vegetable gardening—Juvenile literature. | White House (Washington, D.C.)
Classification: LCC SB321.5.W18 M55 2020 DDC 635—dc23
LC record available at https://lccn.loc.gov/2020005058

ISBN 978-0-316-45857-3

Printed in China

APS

10 9 8 7 6 5 4 3 2 1

 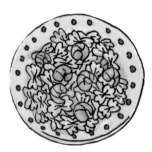 

Michelle's Garden

How the First Lady Planted Seeds of Change

Sharee Miller

Little, Brown and Company

New York Boston

Before Michelle Obama was the First Lady, she was a kid just like you.
She walked to school with her brother, rode her bike, and played outside every day.

Every night her mother made their family a delicious dinner, with at least one vegetable. It tasted so good Michelle would eat it all and ask for...

More, please!

Michelle knew how lucky she was to have a healthy childhood. She wanted the same for her daughters, Malia and Sasha, so that they would grow up strong. Shopping for fresh produce and trying different recipes made them excited to eat new foods.

They even found fun ways to stay active as a family.

They would eat a home-cooked meal together every night. Michelle loved to hear them ask for...

When Michelle became the First Lady of the United States, she hoped to help all kids be healthier. She just needed a way to get them excited about eating more fruits and vegetables.

One day, while walking on the White House lawn, she told President Barack Obama...

1100

She would plant a kitchen garden! There have been other gardens at the White House, but this would be the biggest one ever planted.

It would be large enough to feed everyone in the White House and its guests, and still have plenty more to share. A beautiful garden to inspire others to do the same! There was just one problem....

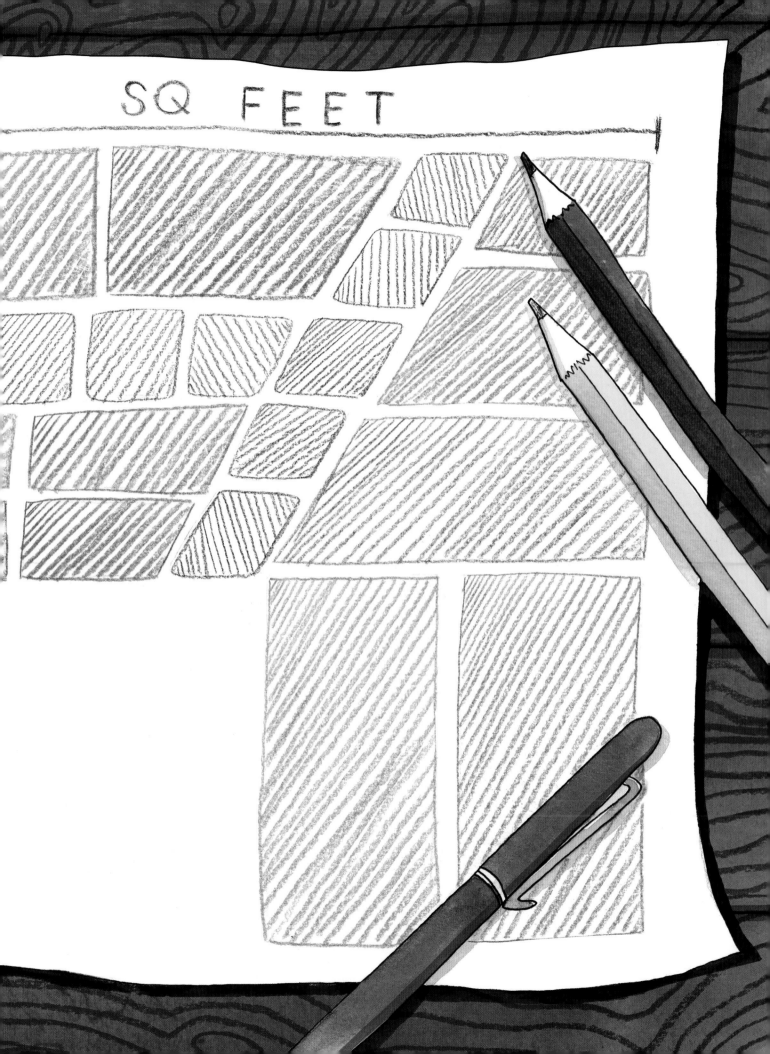

Michelle had never grown
a garden before!
Where should she start?
What tools did she need?
What would she plant?

Everyone needs help when they're trying something new for the first time, so she gathered the White House chefs and gardeners to teach her how to build and care for a garden, and she invited local students to learn along with her.

Together they gathered everything required: soil, shovels, watering cans, and most importantly, seeds.

A garden this big would need lots and lots of seeds.

SHOVEL

GARDEN TROWEL

PRUNERS

SEEDS

HOE

SHEARS

GLOVES

WATERING CAN

FERTILIZER

RAKE

SOIL

WHEELBARROW

GARDEN FORK

They picked a sunny spot on the lawn and got to work!
They moved rocks, dug up the dirt, and fertilized the soil,
then they made a hole for every seed. Each plant had a section,
which was marked with a small sign so they wouldn't forget
what was planted where.

There was no rushing nature, but there were things they could do
to help the garden grow big and strong. They watered the plants
every day, especially when it was hot outside.

They even defended the plants from critters that wanted
to nibble their fruits and veggies before they were ready.

There was a lot to do, so Michelle made sure everyone pitched in, even President Obama.

The little gardeners were nervous.

But all their hard work helped the garden
flourish until it was finally...

harvest day!

Their garden was a success! Everyone gathered onions from the ground, sweet peas off the vine, and berries from the bushes. Some vegetables looked so delicious they didn't make it into the baskets!

Everyone was eager to finally taste all the food they had grown.

Michelle wasn't sure if the students would like all the fruits and vegetables, but they ate every bite and asked for...

So much food had grown from those first small seeds. There was plenty to share, so they donated to people in need.

Michelle's garden started as a small idea and grew into something bigger. She inspired more families, schools, and urban communities across the country to build their own.

Now each seed sprouts new hope and brings us closer to growing a healthier future for kids just like you.

Author's Note

What became of the White House Kitchen Garden? Upon leaving the White House, Michelle took steps to ensure the garden would be protected. She had cement stones put in place to mark a path through the garden, and a wood-and-steel arbor was built to stand above a stone slab that reads "WHITE HOUSE KITCHEN GARDEN—established in 2009 by First Lady Michelle Obama with the hope of growing a healthier nation for our children." This made the garden a permanent fixture on the White House grounds protected by the National Park Service. It was Michelle's actions toward building a brighter future that motivated me to write this book.

The garden grew and changed so much from when it was first planted, and I wanted to be able to capture all the beautiful parts of it. I took some creative license to tell this story, but it was inspired by true events.

My hope is that you will be encouraged to pick up where Michelle Obama and her garden left off. Let's continue to think about what we eat and where it comes from, and make small changes every day to improve our lives. Try a new vegetable or a healthy recipe, or learn to garden! You won't regret it.